GOD IN OUR MIDST

*Prayers and devotions chiefly from
Northern Scotland*

MARTIN REITH

London
SPCK

First published 1975
by the S.P.C.K.
Holy Trinity Church
Marylebone Road
London NW1 4DU

Printed in Great Britain by
Church Army Press, Cowley, Oxford

SBN 281 02834 6

*To my mother
and in memory of my father
who first introduced me
to Christ*

ACKNOWLEDGEMENTS

I am especially grateful to the Reverend G.R.D. McLean for his most generous permission to quote freely from his translations of Gaelic prayers. Also I must thank Sister Caroline, SSM, for supplying me with information about Mother Katharine, and the Reverend Mother Superior for allowing me to include the St Margaret's Fellowship prayer. Too many friends have made useful suggestions with regard to my choice of material, and notes, for me to mention each by name; but I am most grateful to all of them. And to Mrs B. Barron, who so kindly undertook to do all the necessary typing.

Thanks are due to the following for permission to quote from copyright sources:

W & R Chambers Ltd: *Hebridean Altars*, by Alistair Maclean
Peter Davies Ltd: *Reliques of Ancient Scottish Devotion*, by James Cooper
Friends of Aberdeen University Library: *Mystics of the North East*, by G.D. Henderson
Inter-Varsity Press: *Life of God in the Soul of Man*, by Henry Scougal
A & R Milne & Wyllies: *Deeside Tales*, by J.G. Michie
Publications Committee of the Scottish Episcopal Church: *Scottish Prayer Book*
Scottish Academic Press: *Carmina Gadelica, Hymns and Incantations, with Illustrative Notes on Words, Rites, and Customs Dying and Obsolete.*

Biblical quotations from the Revised Standard Version of the Bible, copyrighted 1946 and 1952 by the Division of the Christian Education of the National Council of the Church of Christ in the United States of America, are used by permission.

CONTENTS

	nos.	page
Introduction		3

PRAYERS AND OTHER DEVOTIONS

Preparation	1- 3	11
Morning	4-10	13
Dressing	11-12	16
Kindling the fire	13	17
Grace at meals	14-15	17
On the way to work	16	18
At work	17-23	18
The Christian life	24	21
Through the day	25-32	22
Hymns of praise	33-34	25
Invocation	35-38	26
Devotion	39-46	28
For strength	47-52	31
On a journey	53-54	33
On entering a house	55	33
Blessings	56-58	34
Evening	59-60	35
Forgiveness	61-63	35
Thanksgiving	64-65	36
For the world and family	66-69	37

For the parish	70-71	38
For goodness	72-73	39
For peace	74-75	40
For healing	76-77	40
Smooring the fire	78	41
Light out	79-80	42
Before sleep	81-87	42
Sunday	88	44
Before public worship	89-90	45
Holy Communion	91-93	46
Marriage	94	47
Baptism	95	47
Thanksgiving for children	96	48
For children	97-98	48
Christmas	99-100	49
Holy Week	101-102	50
Easter	103-104	51
Whitsun, or Pentecost	105	52
Communion of saints	106-107	52
For the dying	108-112	53
Eternity	113	55
REFERENCES AND NOTES		59

Introduction

INTRODUCTION

In any age of religious confusion there are those who despair of finding the authentic Christ. Some are haunted by the feeling that nearly two thousand years of Christian experience must be ignored if they themselves are to have a personal encounter with their Saviour, and their inability to distinguish between man-made customs and divine revelation encourages them to reject both.

Meanwhile, as Jesus predicted, only the childlike can enter the kingdom of heaven. All down the ages such men and women have existed, and have come face to face with the living Christ. What was, and often is, obvious to those who live close to nature and in natural integrated communities, is frequently far from clear to the people in 'de-tribalized' cities, where little in life is natural and where sophisticated thinking increasingly threatens to complicate the Christian faith — as expressed in the primitive Creeds — out of all recognition.

The present anthology has been compiled with one aim in view: to set before its readers the best in the religion of many ordinary people who were prepared simply to take Christ at his word; and what ordinary men and women in Scotland have been able to experience for fifteen hundred years is surely not beyond the comprehension of seekers after Christian truth today. For childlike simplicity is a demand of the Saviour as much in a technological as in a pastoral age. Perhaps the poor are blessed and the rich to be pitied — as Jesus said — because wealth diverts attention from the basic necessity of simple trust in God.

The following material has been selected largely from traditional Gaelic prayers. Commenting on one recently published anthology, *Poems of the Western Highlanders*, a reviewer said that 'these immensely various poems breathe the spirit of the ancient Celtic Christianity which . . . held sway for generations in the north before finally yielding first to the more highly organized formalism of Rome, and, much later, to a grim, triumphant Calvinism'. And he went on to remark that they 'are unlike anything else to survive in Christendom'.[1]

A number of people have independently collected traditional prayers in the Gaelic-speaking districts of the Highlands and Islands of Scotland. By far the largest and best-known collection is *Carmina Gadelica*, the lifework of the late Dr Alexander Carmichael. Very recently the Revd G.R.D. McLean has produced new translations of several hundred of these prayers, and his first book — a review of which has just been quoted above — is the chief source for the present anthology.[2]

These poems were part of the great highly-developed oral tradition in Gaelic culture. Many of them breathe the fresh spirit of the early Christian missionaries, and they touch upon every aspect of life. They reveal a firm grasp of the doctrine of the Trinity; and their vivid reflection of the intimate presence of God in, and deep concern with, the smallest details of daily life is allied to a sense of his majesty and supreme greatness. God in fact is intensely real, and very much in our midst.

Used by all classes in that integrated social structure, the clan system, these prayers were often chanted to accompany both private and corporate activities. They were hammered out on the anvil of an exceedingly hard existence, where almost everyone shared in often acute poverty, where famine and disease were regular causes of death, and where violent storms and occasional outbursts of civil unrest added to the general insecurity.

Out of such a background came these poetic prayers. They show the manly simplicity of a boatman in an Atlantic gale, praying in complete trust to 'the king of the elements'. They show the warm tenderness (and even gaiety) of prayers being softly sung on all occasions — whether at the bathing of the baby or at the departure of a son; for poor people, being poor, have no other treasures to divert them from their only earthly possessions, their families. In these prayers it is assumed that the Holy Trinity is all around us and lovingly concerned in everything from neighbours' relationships to herding cattle.

4

A similar assumption is made regarding our Lord's family and friends in the Gospels and his saints of later ages. The prayers reveal a grasp of the wholeness of creation in marked contrast to that disintegrated and unsacramental view of life which is bedevilling much of Christian witness today.

Furthermore, many of these ancient prayers start with a given human situation, and then lead one's thought to God. This is the 'modern' teaching method prescribed by contemporary educationists, and which is being increasingly used by authors of modern devotional books. The Hebridean saying that 'there is a mother's heart in the heart of God'[3] indicates that the reader will find an absence of that exclusive masculinity for which western Christendom, at least, has recently been criticized.[4]

These prayers reflect a civilization in which everything was deliberately orientated towards God.

A long-sustained attack on Gaelic culture has been one of the tragic aspects of Scotland's history. Yet despite this, the fresh, warm, and homely spirit of the early Christian faith, which converted our forefathers and those of the northern and midland English, still persists; and there are those who find themselves very much at home in this expression of Christianity. In this respect it is noteworthy that some of these prayers are still in use in the 'Catholic Isles'[5]; that the new translations from the Gaelic in *Carmina Cadelica* have been made by an Episcopalian; and that much of the spirit of these prayers shines out of the pages of *Hebridean Altars*, which was produced by a Presbyterian.[6]

Any people as racially mixed as the Scots is bound to reveal not only very varied characteristics, but also paradoxes. Perhaps only in our primitive faith – about which we have a vast amount of evidence unparalleled in Christendom – can we really come to grips with that elusive subject, the soul of Scotland. But above all, within the vast collection of traditional Gaelic prayers, we may possess Scotland's distinct and major contribution to Christendom. For 'the Highland way of life' still reflects a scale of values increasingly ignored in the modern world — values which are superbly expressed in the best of these prayers.

The present volume has been prepared chiefly as a book of private devotion; hence the predominant use of prayers in verse rather than in prose form.

In these prayers beginners in the Christian life find elementary concepts of great value; while the most spiritually mature give them the highest praise.[7] Some of the short verses are so condensed that they provide almost inexhaustible material for meditation. It should be borne in mind, however, that every language suffers through translation, and that there is bound to be further difficulty when that translation is rewritten in verse form. The not infrequent beauty of the result is both an indication of the extreme artistic value of many of the originals and of the translator's skill; while a *prayerful* use of these poems will enable the reader to grasp the meaning of those compositions which appear at first sight to be obscure. Above all, many readers should find in these poems a powerful incentive to lead them into the deeper ways of silent prayer.

A little of the following material, however, has been included also for simple corporate use, such as for family prayers. Some readers may well compose prayers according to their own requirements, and numbers 9 and 60 in this collection suggest how traditional material might be modernized.

If some of the prayers and devotional songs reproduced here are of extremely ancient origin, many others have emerged as it were *en route* down the centuries. For this is indeed a living, if not now widespread, tradition to which the contemporary verses of the Revd G.R.D. McLean bear witness. The chants to which they were sung are almost entirely lost, for Dr Carmichael had no recording apparatus in the nineteenth century. In any case much of Gaelic folk-singing — or 'a way of saying it' — is as elusive and variable as it is attractive. The contemporary practice, in homes in some parts of the Hebrides, of singing Gaelic hymns to the tunes of well-known Gaelic songs, illustrates the unity of religion with life which is such an essential feature of this tradition.

To make the present volume as complete and varied as possible, within a small compass, the compiler's notebooks have been scoured for other devotional material from the sixth century to the present day. No claims are made that this is a kind of 'Scottish Treasury', a selection of all the cream of spiritual writing in Scotland. It is simply a collection of devotional material which happens to come almost exclusively from Scotland north and west of the Tay, and which is offered to the public by a priest with the very varied needs of many kinds of people in view.

Inverness, 1975   *MARTIN REITH*

Prayers and other devotions

PREPARATION

1

I am bending low my knee
In the eye of those who see,
   Father, who my life supplied,
   Saviour Son, who for me died,
   Spirit, who hath purified,
      In desire and love to thee.

Grant us, Glory-Saviour dear,
God's affection, love, and fear,
God's will to do always here,
As above in heaven clear
Saints and angels do not cease;
   Day and night give us thy peace,
   Give each day and night thy peace.

Traditional Gaelic,
from Catherine Macintyre, crofter's wife, Barra

2

The Father who created me
With eye benign beholdeth me;
The son who dearly purchased me
With eye divine enfoldeth me;
The Spirit who so altered me
With eye refining holdeth me:
   In friendliness and love the Three
   Behold me when I bend the knee.

O God, through thine Anointed One,
The fulness of our needs be done —
   Grant us towards God the love ordained,
   Grant us towards man the love unfeigned,
   Grant us the smile of God's good face,

Grant us God's wisdom and God's grace;
Grant us to fear and reverence still,
Grant in the world to do thy will,
As done in heaven by saintly hands.
And myriad of angelic bands;
    Each day and night, each dawn and fall,
    Grant us in kindness, Lord of all,
    Thy nature's tincture at our call.

Traditional Gaelic,
from Ann Macdonald, crofter's daughter, Lochaber

3

O God, do thou hearken unto my prayer,
My earnest petition come to thee where
I know that thou hearest with loving care
As though with mine eyes I beheld thee there.

Upon my heart I am setting a bit,
A bit on my thoughts undisciplined sit,
A bit on my lips I securely fit,
And for safety's sake it is double-knit.

But thou God of life thyself, sanctified,
Be at my breast, at my back, at my side,
To me thou a star, to me thou a guide,
From my life's inflowing to ebbing tide.

Traditional Gaelic,
from Catherine Macdonald, cottar, Barra

MORNING

4

When morning in russet and saffron clad
Is mantling the hills in a dew-soft plaid,
To the song of the moorland two-wings glad
    Let my heart upraise;

When light creeps in through the chinks of the door,
When the mist ascends from the mountain floor,
When the ocean shimmers like burnished ore,
    Let me give the praise.

O God of the morning, Christ of the hills,
O Spirit, who all the firmament fills,
O Trinity blest, who all goodness wills,
    Keep us all our days.

G.R.D. McLean

5

Let thanks, O God, be unto thee,

From yesterday who broughtest me
The morning of today to see,
Joy everlasting to earn whole
With good intention for my soul.
For every gift of peace to me,
Thoughts, words, deeds, and desires from thee
Each one bestowed, I dedicate.
And I beseech, I supplicate
That thou may'st keep me from offence,
Tonight my aiding and defence,

For the sake of thy wounding red,
With thine offering of grace outspread.

Let thanks, O God, be unto thee.

Traditional Gaelic,
from Mary Macinnes, cottar, North Uist

6

Though the dawn breaks cheerless on this isle today,
my spirit walks upon a path of light.
    For I know my greatness.
Thou hast built me a throne within thy heart.
I dwell safely within the circle of thy care.
I cannot for a moment fall out of thine everlasting arms.
I am on my way to thy glory.

Alistair Maclean

7

O God, who from last night's sweet rest dost me convey
Unto the light of joy which is today,
From the new light of day be thou bringing me
Unto the guiding light of eternity.

Traditional Gaelic,
from a lighthouse keeper,
Heisgir nam Manach, North Uist (adapted)

8

My prayer to thee, O God, pray I this day,
Voice I this day in thy mouth's voicing way,
As hold the men of heaven this day I hold,
Spend I this day as spends thine own household,

Under thy laws, O God, this day I go,
As saints in heaven pass pass I this day so.

Each day thy mercies' source let me recall,
Gentle, gen'rous bestowing on me all;
Each day in love to thee more full be I
For love to me that thou didst amplify.

From thee it came, each thing I have received,
From love it comes, each thing my hope conceived,
Thy bounty gives each thing that gives me zest,
Of thy disposing each thing I request.

God holy, loving Father, of the word
Everlasting, this loving prayer be heard;
Understanding lighten, my will enfire,
Begin my doing and my love inspire,
My weakness strengthen, enfold my desire.

Cleanse heart, faith confirm, sanctify my soul,
Circle my body, and my mind keep whole;
As from my mouth my prayer upriseth clear,
May I feel in my heart that thou art here.

And, Father beloved, grant thou that to me,
From whom each thing that is outfloweth free,
No tie too strict, no tie too dear between
Myself and this beneath-world here be seen.

Father, Son, Spirit, Holy Trinity,
Three in One Person and the One in Three,
Infinite and perfect, world without end,
Changeless through endless life, let praise ascend.

Traditional Gaelic

9

O God, Father, Son, and Holy Spirit,
we thank you for last night's rest and for bringing us
safely to the morning joy of this new day.
Lead and inspire us in all that we do;
strengthen our trust in you;
fill us with your love for everyone,
and from the light of this day bring us clean from sin
to the full light of your everlasting presence:
One God, now and for ever, Amen.

10

Beloved, go and live thy life in the spirit of my dying,
                              in righteousness and love;
then truly shalt thou share my victory and taste my peace.

Hebridean Altars

DRESSING

11

Bless to me, O God, my body and my soul;
Bless to me, O God, belief, condition whole;
Bless to me, O God, my heart, my speaking too,
And bless to me, O God, the things my hands do.

Traditional Gaelic,
from Catherine Maclennan, crofter, Moydart

12

Grant to our souls, we pray thee, thy merciful aiding,
covering them with the shadow of thy wing even as we clothe
our bodies.

Traditional Gaelic

KINDLING THE FIRE

13

This morning I will kindle the fire upon my hearth
Before the holy angels who stand about my path.

God, a love-flame kindle in my heart to neighbours all,
To foe, to friend, to kindred, to brave, to knave, to thrall,
O Son of lovely Mary, from lowliest thing on earth,
To the Name that highest is and of the greatest worth.
    O Son of lovely Mary, from lowliest thing on earth,
    To the Name that highest is and of the greatest worth.

Traditional Gaelic,
from Mary Maclellan, crofter's wife, North Uist

GRACE AT MEALS

14

We are God's guests and 'tis he who keeps the
generous table.

A Lewis man

15

All thanks and praise and worship be unto thee, O God,
for all that thou hast given unto us,
and as thou hast given the life of our body to win the food
of this world, so grant us the life eternal to show forth
thy glory, through Jesus Christ our Lord.

Traditional Gaelic,
from Malcolm Macmillan, merchant, Benbecula

ON THE WAY TO WORK

16

'Tis God's will I would do,
My own will I would rein;

Would give to God his due,
From my own due refrain;

God's path I would pursue,
My own path would disdain.

Traditional Gaelic

AT WORK

17

Helmsman	Be the ship blest.
Crew	By God the Father blest.
Helmsman	Be the ship blest.
Crew	And by God the Son blest.
Helmsman	Be the ship blest.
Crew	By God the Spirit blest.

18

All   God the Father,
                  And God the Son,
                  God the Spirit,
                      Blessing give best,
                      Be the ship blest.

                  Being of all,
                  The king of all,
                  Spirit of all,
                      Over our head eternal fall,
                      Near to us sure for evermore.

Traditional Gaelic,
from Archibald Maclellan, shipmaster, South Uist

18

Even though the day be laden and my task dreary and my
strength small, a song keeps singing in my heart.
For I know that I am thine.

    I am part of thee. Thou art kin to me and all my times
are in thy hand.

Alistair Maclean

19

No one ever appealed to her for help in vain, for helping others,
however varied their needs, and teaching, were almost a passion
with her. She spent herself in the service of others, and
endeared herself to all who knew her. Self seemed eliminated,
and all self-consciousness was absent from her work, so keen
was her interest in it. She was most practical and matter-of-fact,
saw the bright side of things and made the best of them, often
turning others' gloom into laughter. Simplicity and straight-
forwardness were guiding principles of her life.

Of Katharine Ogilvie, Aberdeen, 1854-1932

20

O thou king above of virtues and power,
Thy blessing for fishing upon us shower.

Traditional Gaelic,
from Angus Maclellan, cooper, Benbecula

21

Be blessing, O God, my little cow,
    And be blessing, O God, my intent;
O God, my partnership blessing thou,
    And my hands that to milking are sent.

Traditional Gaelic

22

My Chief of generous heroes, bless
    My loom and all things near to me,
Bless me in all my busy-ness,
    Keep me for life safe-dear to thee.

Traditional Gaelic,
from Donald Macintyre, catechist, Benbecula

23

Seven times a day, as I work upon this hungry farm,
I say to thee,
    'Lord, why am I here? What is there here to stir my gifts
to growth? What great thing can I do for others —
I who am captive to this dreary toil?'

And seven times a day thou answerest,
   'I cannot do without thee.
Once did my Son live thy life, and by his faithfulness did show
my mind, my kindness, and my truth to men. But now he is
come to my side, and thou must take his place.'

Hebridean Altars

THE CHRISTIAN LIFE

24

When thou turn'st away from ill,
Christ is this side of thy hill.

When thou turnest toward good,
Christ is walking in thy wood.

When thy heart says, 'Father, pardon!'
Then the Lord is in thy garden.

When stern duty wakes to watch,
Then his hand is on thy latch.

But when hope thy song doth rouse,
Then the Lord is in the house.

When to love is all thy wit,
Christ doth at thy table sit.

When God's will is thy heart's pole,
Then is Christ thy very soul.

George MacDonald, 1824-1905

25

Saviour and friend, how wonderful art thou!
My companion upon the changeful way. The comforter of
   its weariness.
My guide to the eternal town. The welcome at its gate.

Alistair Maclean

26

How wonderful is thy friendliness toward me!
How deep! How unchanging.
Give me a grace to pass it on.

Alistair Maclean

27

I saw a Highlander carefully, and with patient kindness,
carry a poor wounded soldier on his back into a house,
where he left him, with a sixpence to pay his charges.

After the battle of Prestonpans 1745

28

Thou King of the moon and of the sun,
   Of the stars thou lov'd and fragrant King,
Thou thyself knowest our needs each one,
   O merciful God of everything.

Each day that our moving steps we take,
   Each hour of awakening, when we know
The dark distress and sorrow we make
   To the King of hosts who loved us so;

Be with us through the time of each day,
  Be with us through the time of each night,
Be with us ever each night and day,
  Be with us ever each day and night.

Traditional Gaelic

29

O God, do thou
  steer with thy wisdom,
  correct with thy justice,
  assist with thy mercy,
  and protect with thy strength.

Traditional Gaelic,
from Janet Macisaac, crofter's wife, South Uist

30

I am serene because I know thou lovest me.
Because thou lovest me, naught can move me from my peace.
Because thou lovest me, I am as one to whom all good has come.

Alistair Maclean

31

As the hand is made for holding and the eye for seeing,
  thou hast fashioned me for joy.

Share with me the vision that shall find it everywhere:
  in the wild violet's beauty;
  in the lark's melody;
  in the face of a steadfast man;

in a child's smile;
in a mother's love;
in the purity of Jesus.

Alistair Maclean

32

There is no plant in all the land
    But blooms replete with thy virtue,
Each form in all the sweeping strand
    With joy replete thou dost endue,
        O Jesu, Jesu, Jesu,
        Unto whom all praise is due.

All life that is within the sea,
    In river every dwelling thing,
All in the firmament that be
    Thy goodness overflowing sing,
        O Jesu, Jesu, Jesu,
        Unto whom all praise is due.

Each single star fixed in the sky,
    Each bird arising on the wing,
They that beneath the sun do lie,
    Thy goodness all proclaiming sing,
        O Jesu, Jesu, Jesu,
        Unto whom all praise is due.

Traditional Gaelic,
from Mary Ferguson, cottar, Harris

24

33

O God, thou art the Father
    Of all that have believed:
From whom all hosts of angels
    Have life and power received.
O God, thou art the maker
    Of all created things,
The righteous judge of judges,
    The almighty king of kings.

High in the heav'nly Zion
    Thou reignest God adored;
And in the coming glory
    Thou shalt be sovereign lord.
Beyond our ken thou shinest,
    The everlasting light;
Ineffable in loving,
    Unthinkable in might.

Thou to the meek and lowly
    Thy secrets dost unfold;
O God, thou doest all things,
    All things both new and old.
I walk secure and blessèd
    In every clime or coast,
In name of God the Father,
    And Son, and Holy Ghost.

St Columba, 521-97

34

Child in the manger,
    Infant of Mary:
Outcast and stranger,

Lord of all!
Child who inherits
    All our transgressions,
All our demerits
    On him fall.

Once the most holy
    Child of salvation
Gently and lowly
    Lived below;
Now, as our glorious
    Mighty Redeemer,
See him victorious
    O'er each foe.

Prophets foretold him,
    Infant of wonder;
Angels behold him
    On his throne;
Worthy our Saviour
    Of all their praises;
Happy for ever
    Are his own.

Mary Macdonald, 1817-90

INVOCATION

35

God with me lying down,
God with me rising up:

God with me in each ray of light,
Nor I a ray of joy without him,
    Nor one ray without him.

God with me protecting,
The Lord with me directing,
The Spirit with me strengthening,
    For ever and for evermore,

    Ever and evermore, Amen.
    Chief of chiefs, Amen.

Traditional Gaelic,
from Mary Macrae, dairywoman, Harris

36

God over me, God under me,
God before me, God behind me,
    I on thy path, O God,
    Thou, O God, in my steps.

Traditional Gaelic,
from Catrine Mackintosh, cottar, North Uist

37

As thine angels fair, untiring,
    As thy saints, household entire,
They in heav'n above desiring,
    So on earth may I desire,
    With Holy Ghost aflame in fire.

Traditional Gaelic

38

God to enfold,
God to surround,
God in speech-told,
God my thought-bound.

God when I sleep,
God when I wake,
God my watch-keep,
God my hope-sake.

God my life-whole,
God lips apart,
God in my soul,
God in my heart.

God Wine and Bread,
God in my death,
God my soul-thread,
God ever breath.

Traditional Gaelic

DEVOTION

39

There is no secret — only — only
I am always at his feet, and he is
always in my heart.

A Hebridean princess

40

May the blessed Virgin Mary
And the fragrant Branch of Glory
Be in my heart and soul always,
To have my worship and my praise,
O in my heart and soul always.

Traditional Gaelic,
from Ann Macdonald, crofter's daughter, Lochaber

41

Wilt thou not yield me vision,
Lord of grace,
Of that vast realm
Of unhorizoned space
Which is thy heart
That heart-room makes for all?

Alistair Maclean

42

A verdict in the old city slums on one who reflected the love of Christ:
'Send me Sister Katharine; she does something to me — her heart is as big as Aberdeen.'

Katharine Ogilvie, 1854-1932

43

I am giving thee worship with my whole life every hour,
    I am giving thee assent with my whole power,
With my fill of tongue's utterance I am giving thee praise,
    I am giving thee honour with my whole lays.

I am giving thee loving with my devotion's whole art,
    I am giving kneeling with my whole desire,
I am giving thee liking with my whole beating of heart,
    I am giving affection with my sense-fire;

I am giving mine existing with my mind and its whole,
    O God of all gods, I am giving my soul.

Traditional Gaelic,
from Mary Gillies, crofter, Morar

44

With Jesus to find restfulness
In the blest habitation of peace,
In the paradise of gentleness,
In the fairy-bower of release
    Mercy-arrayed.

Traditional Gaelic

45

May he alone be our love, our joy and our all! May his holy
presence be our continual entertainment and delight.

In the world, saith he, ye shall have trouble, but
in me ye shall have peace; be of good comfort,
for I have overcome the world.

He knows and through his grace we know that we are nothing
and can do nothing; but we trust that he will be our king, our
strength, our wisdom and righteousness; and that he will give
us not only to believe in his name but to suffer for his truth,
and through the power of his Holy Spirit to rejoice continually
under all his providences concerning us.

James Keith, doctor
Aberdeen and London, 1715

46

I find thee throned in my heart, my lord Jesus.
It is enough.
I know that thou art throned in heaven.
My heart and heaven are one.

Alistair Maclean

FOR STRENGTH

47

As the rain hides the stars, as the autumn mist hides the hills,
as the clouds veil the blue of the sky, so the dark
happenings of my lot hide the shining of thy face from me.
Yet, if I may hold thy hand in the darkness, it is enough.
Since I know that, though I may stumble in my going,
thou dost not fall.

Alistair Maclean

48

An elderly, almost lifelong invalid, describing an operation
which had been done to her foot without anaesthetic, said, very
simply, 'I put out my hand and took Christ's, and it was all
right'.

Grace Reith
Aberdeen and London, 1878-1965

49

Your own experience convinces you that our life is in all
respects a continual warfare, that everywhere and in all estates
we must be proved and tried both from without and within.

This is the lot of a true disciple, and I'm sure 'tis a happy one
when improved according to our Lord's intention. Nothing
then that happens must disturb or disquiet us. . .

May it please him to increase our faith and strengthen our
dependence on him.

James Keith, doctor
Aberdeen and London, 1713

50

In the name of the God of life above,
In the holy name of the Christ of love,
In the name of the Holy Spirit-Dove,
    The Three-One together my strength enough.

Traditional Gaelic,
from Roderick Macdonald, Tiree

51

Thy will be done in me.

Thou art my father. I am thy child. Whatever comes to me,
therefore, must be of thy love's sending.

Father! thou wilt not hurt thine own child.

Alistair Maclean

52

Thou art our father, therefore our strength and light.
Of which we, who are now at the chair of thy grace,
ask for a portion, so that we may have power to do thy will,
        even though it be a cross.

A widowed mother in Mull

ON A JOURNEY

53

Who are the ones at my helm-tiller near?
    Peter and Paul and John Baptist are they;
At my helm the Christ is sitting to steer,
    The wind from the south making our way.

Traditional Gaelic,
from Alexander Matheson, shipmaster, Lochalsh

54

May God shield us by each sheer drop,
May Christ keep us on each rock-path,
May the Spirit fill us on each bare slope,
    as we cross hill and plain,
Who live and reign
One God for ever. Amen.

Traditional Gaelic

ON ENTERING A HOUSE

55

Peace of God be unto you,
Peace of Christ be unto you,
Peace of Spirit be unto you,
Peace be to your children too,
To your children and to you.

Traditional Gaelic

BLESSINGS

56

The blessing of God be upon you, that good come to you;
The blessing of Christ be upon you, that good be done to you;
The blessing of the Holy Ghost be yours, that good be the
course of your life,
each day of your arising, each night of your lying down,
for evermore, Amen.

Traditional Gaelic

57

The God of life with guarding hold you,
The loving Christ with guarding fold you,
The Holy Spirit, guarding, mould you,
each night of life to aid, enfold you,
each day and night of life uphold you.

Traditional Gaelic

58

The Father eternal's shield thine,
Upon his own lit altar-shrine;
The Father's shield always be thine,
Eternal from his altar-shrine
Lit up by gold taperflame-shine.

A traditional Gaelic mother's farewell

EVENING

59

When the shadows fall upon hill and glen:
and the bird music is mute:
when the silken dark is a friend:
and the river sings to the star,

    ask thyself, brother, ask thyself, sister,
    the question thou alone hast power to answer:

        O King and Saviour of men,
        what is thy gift to me? and do I use it to thy pleasing?

Alistair Maclean

60

O God of all life,
        thank you for looking after us today,
        for all your gifts to us, and joys.

Bless us this night with your forgiveness.

Bless this house with peace,
and all our dear ones, wherever they are,

    for Jesus' sake, Amen.

FORGIVENESS

61

Rejoice therefore, O my soul, for God wills thy reconciling;
seize hold upon his outstretched hand to tell thee of a reconciling
love.

Traditional Gaelic,
Ann Macdonald, widow, Lochaber

O God of life and tenderness,
With thy forgiveness do thou bless,
In each my word of wickedness,
In each my oath's untruthfulness,
In each my deed of foolishness,
And in my speech of emptiness.

Traditional Gaelic

Grant thou unto me, O God, to show
    A repentance unreserved, sincere;
Grant thou unto me, O God, to know
    Repentance wholehearted, without fear;
Grant thou unto me, O God, to owe
    A repentance lasting, to thee dear.

Traditional Gaelic,
from Ann Macdonald, Lochaber

THANKSGIVING

O God, for ever praise be to thee

    For the blessings thou bestow'st on me —
    For my food, my work, my health, my speech,
    For all the good gifts bestowed on each,

O God, for ever praise be to thee.

Traditional Gaelic,
from Mary Macdonald, Lochaber

65

O grant thou to us, O God of our peace,
Whate'er be our loss a thankful heart,
To obey thy laws here below nor cease,
To enjoy thee when yon we depart.

Traditional Gaelic,
from Mary Macdonald, Lochaber

FOR THE WORLD AND FAMILY

66

They lived together nearly half a century on this part of
Deeside, the best of parents, giving a good example in every way,
and serving to the utmost of their power all who stood in need.

Of Charles Gordon of Abergeldie, who died in 1796,
and his wife Alison Hunter

67

God bless the world and all that in it dwell,
God bless my partner, children dear as well.

Traditional Gaelic,
from Isabel Mackintosh, crofter's wife, Lochaber

68

Bless, O our God, the household folk,
According as Lord Jesus spoke;
Bless, O our God, the family,
As offered it should be to thee.

Traditional Gaelic,
from Catherine Macphie, cottar, South Uist

69

The dwelling, O God, by thee be blest,
And each one who here this night doth rest;
My dear ones, O God, bless thou and keep
In every place where they are asleep.

Traditional Gaelic

FOR THE PARISH

70

God bless our church and parish, and prosper all our attempts
to be faithful and to draw others to you, for Jesus Christ's
sake, Amen.

71

O Christ, ascending to Father's right hand,
O Christ, outsending the missionary band,
O Christ, attending the prayer, by me stand
 All my nights and my days.

O Spirit of wisdom, Spirit of might,
O Spirit of counsel, strength for the fight,
O Spirit of fear, understanding's sight,
 And where godliness stays:

O Spirit of faith, the descending dove,
O Spirit of hope, outpoured from above,
O Spirit, infusing and breathing love,
 Lighten, set me ablaze.

G.R.D. McLean

FOR GOODNESS

72

Deliver us, O Lord, from evil.

O Lord Jesu Christ, keep us always in every good work.

O God, the fountain and author of all good things,
empty us of vices,
    and fill us with good virtues;
        through thee, Christ Jesus.

Book of Deer, 9th century

73

That thou wouldest give us perseverance in good works:
    we beseech thee to hear us . . .
That thou wouldest grant us that charity which the world
                            cannot give:
    we beseech thee to hear us.

    Christ is victor; Christ is king; Christ is lord of all.

    Thou, O Christ, grant to us thy grace.
    Thou, O Christ, give to us joy and peace.
    Thou, O Christ, grant to us life and salvation.

Almighty and most bountiful God we humbly implore thy
Majesty, that . . . thou wouldest grant to us pardon and
forgiveness of all our sins, the increase of thy heavenly grace,
and thine effectual help against all snares of our enemies
visible and invisible, inasmuch as our hearts also are given up
wholly to thy commandments, so that, at the last, after this
mortal life is ended, we may see the face and glory of thy
saints in the kingdom of God, and be counted worthy to
rejoice with them in our most glorious lord Jesus Christ our
redeemer;   to whom be glory and honour and power and

dominion, with the Father and the Holy Ghost, throughout all ages.   Amen.

Litany of Dunkeld, 9th century

FOR PEACE

74

O God, grant us thy peace,
the peace of men also,
the peace of St Columba, the kind,
and of St Mary mild, the loving one,
and of Christ, the king of human heart.

Traditional Gaelic

75

Almighty Father, I offer all the trials of my daily life in union with the sacrifice of our Lord on the cross. Teach me to bear them gladly for the intention of bringing souls to thee.

Prayer of the Fellowship of St Margaret of Scotland

FOR HEALING

76

May God, my dear, be thy healing one;

> I set my hand upon thee this day
> In name of Father,

In name of Son,
In name of Spirit of power, I pray,
Three Persons who compass thee alway.

Traditional Gaelic,
from Ian Mackay, crofter, Kinlochewe

77

O God of all grace, my body satisfy;
O Christ of the Passion, satisfy my soul;
O Spirit of wisdom, grant light to me to lie,
And restore to me repose, making me whole.

Traditional Gaelic,
from Mary Macrae, cottar, Kintail

SMOORING THE FIRE

78

I will keep in and smoor the hearth
    As Mary would smoor the peat;
Bride and Mary making a path
    Round floor and fire with their feet,
        The protection to fall
        On the household, on all.

Who is out on the grassy lawn?
    Mary sun-white, her Son there;
God's angel spake, God's mouth hath sworn;
    Angels of promise, flame-fair
        Watch the hearth, till white day
        On the ash-glow doth play.

Traditional Gaelic,
from Catherine Macpharlan, soldier's wife, Barra

41

LIGHT OUT

79

'There need be no twilight. A man has Christ. Is he not the truth?' he whispered. 'Is he not the light? Is he not the keeper of the treasure we seek so blindly?'

An Islesman

80

Light of lights, take darkness' part
From thy place into my heart;
Spirit's wisdom music start
From my Saviour in my heart.

Traditional Gaelic

BEFORE SLEEP

81

In thy name, O Jesu, who wast crucified,
　　Down I lay myself for my repose;
In sleep far-away do thou watch by my side,
　　In thy one hand do thou hold me close;
　　　　In sleep far-away do thou watch by my side,
　　　　In thy one hand do thou hold me close.

Thy blessing, O my Christ, be upon me laid,
　　Unto me a buckler shielding be,
In the sinking bogland to my steps give aid,
　　To eternal life be leading me;
　　　　In the sinking bogland to my steps give aid,
　　　　To eternal life be leading me.

Traditional Gaelic,
from Peggy Maccormick, crofter and nurse, South Uist

82

As is due I am laying me down tonight,
   The Christ my friend, Son of ringleted Maid,
Father of glory my friend, of gracious light,
   The Holy Spirit my friend, of mighty aid.

Traditional Gaelic,
from John Macinnes, crofter, South Uist

83

With evil I will not lie down,
   Nor shall evil lie down with me,
But with God I will lay me down,
   God himself will lie down with me.

Traditional Gaelic,
from Archibald Currie, shoemaker, South Uist

84

I am tired and I a stranger,
Lead thou me to the land of angels;
For me it is time to go home,
To the court of Christ, to the peace of heaven.

Traditional Gaelic,
from Isabel Mackintosh, crofter's wife, Lochaber

85

God, give us rest, our eyelids sealed,
Thy rock of covenant our shield.

Traditional Gaelic

43

Father eternal, chief of mankind,
Enwrap my body and soul entwined,
Safeguard me tonight in thy love shrined,
The saints' aid tonight my shelter kind.

Traditional Gaelic,
from Mary Gillies, crofter, Morar

87

I am going now into the sleep,
    Be it that I in health shall wake;
If death be to me in deathly sleep,
Be it that in thine own arm's keep,
    O God of grace, to new life I wake;
O be it in thy dear arm's keep,
    O God of grace, that I shall awake!

Traditional Gaelic,
from Donald Macdonald, crofter, Benbecula

SUNDAY

88

On God's holy Sunday do thou mind
To give thine heart to all mankind,
Love to father and mother to bring,
More than to other person or thing.

Despise not the weak or poor at all,
Do thou not covet large or small,
For semblance of evil make no place,
Give thou ne'er nor merit disgrace.

The ten commandments God-given of old
Con and know early, proven gold,

Direct in the king of life believe,
Idol-worship behind thee leave.

To thine own chieftain be clansman true,
To thine own chief the service due,
True to thyself with a firm belief,
True through each mood to thy High Chief.

On no man pass the sentence malign,
Lest malison in turn be thine;
Take the step of God's Anointed-One,
Journey by sea or land begun,
The very step of God's own Son.

Traditional Gaelic,
from Ian Pearson, cottar, Barra

BEFORE PUBLIC WORSHIP

89

O Lord, I am now in thy house of prayer; assist, I pray thee,
and accept of my services! Enable me and all who shall this day
meet in thy name, to worship thee in spirit and in truth! Let
thy Holy Spirit help our infirmities, and dispose our hearts to
seriousness, attention and devotion: and grant that we may
improve this opportunity to the honour of thy holy name, and
the benefit of our souls, through Jesus Christ our Lord, Amen.

Alexander Christie, Keith, 1791

90

O God, this is your house: help us to remember that
you are here with us, and to worship you, for Jesus Christ's
                                                              sake.

From CSG leaflet 'Holy Communion'

HOLY COMMUNION

91

And certainly the neglect or careless performance of this duty, is one of the chief causes that be-dwarfs our religion, and makes us to continue of so low a size.

Henry Scougal, professor, Aberdeen, 1650-78

92

God grant me bread and wine,
The Christ-life that is thine,
Partaking of it mine,
The sustenance divine.

G.R.D. McLean

93

Refreshed with the body and blood of Christ, we give thanks unto thee, O Lord, at all times ... both now and ever, world without end, Amen! Refreshed with the body and blood of Christ, we praise thee, O Lord.

We render thanks unto thee, O God, through whom we have celebrated these holy mysteries: and from thee we ask the gifts of holiness; have mercy upon us, O Lord, saviour of the world: who reignest through ages of ages. Amen.

Book of Deer, 9th century

MARRIAGE

94

The beauty of God is in thy face,
The Son of God is protecting thee
From the wicked ones of world-disgrace,
The king of the stars thy vanguard be.

Since 'tis Mary and Jesus her son
Who set this pleasantness in thy face,
May mild honey's taste thy lips be on
And on each word thou speakest in grace,
To simple, to noble, high and low,
To men, tender women, from this day
Till thine ending day relying so
On the Belov'd and the pow'rs of aye,
On the life-God and his Son-shield-stay.

Traditional Gaelic

BAPTISM

95

Yours be the blessing of God and the Lord,
The perfect Spirit his blessing afford,
The Trinity's blessing on you outpoured
With gentle and gen'rous shedding abroad,
So gently gen'rously for you unstored.

Traditional Gaelic

THANKSGIVING FOR CHILDREN

96

I send my heart to thee in thanks for these little ones: for the strange uprising of happiness that comes to me as my eye follows them.

Sweet is the music of their wind-borne laughter, yea, sweeter than all musics.

I listen to them, and am one with the mavis and the dawn and the flower.

And then I wonder what thy thought is of them — thy children. Yet I need not wonder. For I look upward and lo! thou art leaning out over the window of heaven, and thou art smiling.

An eighty-year-old man

FOR CHILDREN

97

Thou seest me, Father, stand before my cottage door, watching my little ones at play.

O thou, to whom to love and to be are one, hear my faith-cry for them who are more thine than mine.

Give each of them what is best for each. I cannot tell what it is. But thou knowest. I only ask thou love them and keep them with the loving and keeping thou dost show to Mary's son and thine.

A Hebridean mother

The peace of God and of Christ and of the Holy Spirit be upon
us and upon our children, us and our children, for evermore,

                                                            Amen.

Traditional Gaelic

CHRISTMAS

99

With heavenly music down he came
Forth from the Father of his name,
While harp and lyre in song acclaim
    Applauding him.

O Christ, thou refuge of my love,
Why lift not I thy fame above?
When saints and angels full enough
    Are songing thee.

Traditional Gaelic,
from Flora Macdougal, cottar, Barra

100

Heavenly joy and peace upon earth,
    Behold his feet have reached the place;
O worship the king, hail the Lamb's birth,
    King of the virtues, Lamb of grace,
Ocean and earth to him alit
As he doeth it,
    Ho! ro! joy let there be!

Traditional Gaelic,
from Angus Gunn, cottar, Lewis

HOLY WEEK

101

He who so calmly, so calmly rode
    The little ass so fair of gait,
Who healed each hurt and each wound of blood
    That is each generation's fate:

Joy he gave to the outcast and sad,
    To restless and tired he gave rest,
Bond and unruly their freedom had,
    Old and young in the land were blest.

Traditional Gaelic,
from Isabel MacEachainn, cottar, Mull

102

Tonight the anguish hanging is hailed,
The anguish cross to which Christ was nailed,
Christ is the Priest who this eve prevailed,
    Christ is the Priest of love.

Noble the gift! and noble the plight!
Noble the man of this evening's night!
Christ is the Priest above us aright,
    Christ is the Priest of the bread.

Upon this knoll an assemblage great,
Man to man with no envious hate,
Christ is the Priest above us in state,
    Christ is the Priest of the wine.

Traditional Gaelic,
from Duncan Maclellan, crofter, South Uist

EASTER

103

Where two or three together are
In pasture isle or shieling far
    The Lord Christ there
    Doth hear the prayer;
        For in their midst he doth abide,
        Is by their side.

G.R.D. McLean

104

I climb a secret hill
Each Easter morn;
Not for to breathe my fill
Of wonder born
Anew on such a day;
But, more to hear
A trump immortal sound
Within mine ear,
A noise of viols
And a beat of drums,
Bugles that cry,
'He did not die
For aye;
Behold he comes,
Victor from death's
Red fray'.

Alistair Maclean

WHITSUN OR PENTECOST

105

O Holy Ghost
Of power the most,
Come down upon us and subdue;
From glory's place
In heaven space,
Thy light of brilliance shed as dew.

Traditional Gaelic

COMMUNION OF SAINTS

106

To be by one's self in a foreign town, surrounded by strange
faces, seems to increase one's sense of dependence upon God,
and the isolation from one's fellows, brings more before one
the fellow-citizenship with the saints, and with the household
of God, which we are too apt to forget in the midst of the
congenial fellowship of those we love here below.

Alexander Penrose Forbes, Dundee, 1817-75

107

O God the king of saints, we praise and magnify thy holy name
for all thy servants who have finished their course in thy faith
and fear,
for the blessed Virgin Mary, for the holy patriarchs, prophets,
apostles and martyrs, and for all other thy righteous servants;
and we beseech thee that, encouraged by their example,

strengthened by their fellowship, and aided by their prayers, we may attain unto everlasting life; through the merits of thy son Jesus Christ our Lord.

Scottish Prayer Book 1929

FOR THE DYING

108

O sleep thou, sleep, with thy sorrow away and sleep,
 O sleep thou, sleep, with thy sorrow away and sleep,
O sleep thou, sleep, with they sorrow away and sleep;
 O sleep, thou sweet one, the Rock of the fold thy keep.

The great sleep of Jesus, the sleep surpassing deep,
 The sleep of Jesu's wound, of Jesus sorrow-pressed,
The young sleep of Jesus, Jesu's restoring sleep,
 The kiss-sleep of Jesus with peace and glory blest.

Death's shadow, O my dear, upon thy face doth lie,
 But the Jesus of grace about thee hath his hand;
To thy pains be health from the Trinity anigh,
 Calm is in Christ's mind as before thee he doth stand.

Tranquil be thy sleep, the sleep of tranquillity,
 Guided be thy sleep, the sleep of the guided way,
Loving be thy sleep, the sleep of loving for thee;
 In the Lord Chief of life, O sleep, my love, for aye,
 And in the God of life, O sleep, my love, for aye.

Traditional Gaelic

109

I do not think that I shall fear thee when I see thee face to face. For I call to mind my father, he who was the true man

53

and the kind. And my mother, the pure one, out of whose
heart flowed the waters of healing. And, as I think of them, my
pulses beat with joy and I cry to thee, Father, and say: 'Thou
art more and tenderer than they.' Therefore when I am come
into the court of thy presence I know that thou wilt look upon
me with my father's eyes and with my mother's pity and that
thou wilt draw me to thy breast.

Alistair Maclean

110

As the moorland pool images the sun, so in our hours of self-
giving thou shinest on us, and we mirror thee to men. But of the
other land, our heaven to be, we have no picture at all. Only
we know that thou art there. And Jesus the door and the
welcome of each faithful one.

Alistair Maclean

111

Grant us therefore a death of unction and of repentance,
of rejoicing and of peace,   of grace and of forgiveness,
a death which gives heaven and life with Christ,
in whose name we ask this.   Amen.

Traditional Gaelic

112

Heavenly light directs my feet,
The music of the skies gives peace to my soul,
Alone I am under the wing of the rock,
Angels of God calling me home.

Traditional Gaelic,
from Peter MacDonald, Glencoe

ETERNITY

113

As it was, as it is, and as it shall be
Evermore, God of grace, God in Trinity!
With the ebb, with the flow, ever it is so,
God of grace, O Trinity, with the ebb and flow.

Traditional Gaelic,
from Alexander Macneill, fish salter, Barra

114

I remember myself, though I was little at the time, when the
Christian folk crowded into one another's houses, telling tales
and histories, invocations and prayers, singing hymns and
songs, runes and lays, sweet, beautiful, and soft.

A crofter's wife, Barra

Reference and Notes

REFERENCES AND NOTES

Numbers in brackets refer to Alexander Carmichael: *Carmina Gadelica, Hymns and Incantations, with Illustrative Notes on Words, Rites and Customs Dying and Obsolete* (Oliver and Boyd, vols. i, ii., 1900, 2nd edn 1928; vol. iii., 1940; vol. iv., 1941).

The reference *Poems* . . . (&c.) implies that the whole poem is reproduced in full; where only part is quoted the reference is 'From *Poems* . . .' (&c.)

Abbreviations

Altars	*Hebridean Altars;* Alistair Maclean (Edinburgh 1937)
Poems	*Poems of the Western Highlanders;* G.R.D. McLean (S.P.C.K. 1961)
Poems II	Vol. II of the above, as yet unpublished

INTRODUCTION

1. *Church Times,* 12 January 1962.

2. *Poems of the Western Highlanders* (S.P.C.K. 1961); copies available from Messrs. James Thin, The Bridges, Edinburgh.

3. *Altars*, p. 92. The author was latterly minister of Daviot.

4. Augustine Morris, Abbot of Nashdom, *Prayer in the 1970s;* copies available from Nashdom Abbey, Burnham, Bucks.

5. See, e.g., Margaret Fay Shaw, *Folksongs and Folklore of South Uist* (London 1955), pp. 19-22.

6. Alistair Maclean, see above.

7. I am much indebted to the teaching of the late Reverend Gilbert Shuldham Shaw on Celtic spirituality.

PRAYERS AND DEVOTIONS

1. From *Poems* 237 [i. p.34-5]. The human spatial conception of heaven being above is regarded as perfectly consistent, in these prayers, with a realization that heaven is all around us. Perhaps what is often believed in this literal age to be inconsistent is only perfectly clear to those who have not lost their sense of the wholeness of life.

59

2. *Poems* 157 [i. 2-3]. (In the last line the word 'spirit' may be used instead of 'tincture'.) The more a person's life is given to God, the more is he likely to become aware that God regards his child 'in friendliness and love'; but see note 47 below.

3. From *Poems* 74 [iii. 70-1]. The warmth and gentleness in religion which is so vividly expressed in these prayers is the result of the strictest self-discipline.

4. *Poems*, p. 75.

5. *Poems* 90 [i. 98-9]. Reminding oneself of the purpose of life, at the beginning of each day, is of great value. In various ways this is done throughout this section of morning prayers.

6. *Altars*, p. 55. As urban, industrial Britain becomes increasingly materialistic and impersonal, it is all the more important to be reminded of the value of simply being a child of God.

7. From *Poems* 434 [i. 32-3]. This verse (slightly modernized) well illustrates the principle of using an everyday circumstance to lead the mind on to religious truth.

8. From *Poems* 94 [iii. 58-61]. God is seen as the source of all goodness, and therefore his presence adds to one's enjoyment and gives zest. In view of consistent advice given in the spiritual classics, the word 'feel' in the fifth stanza needs perhaps to be qualified. Religion, like life, cannot depend on mere feelings; yet the desire for awareness of God is perfectly natural. See note, reference 51. Another important matter to which this prayer refers is the fact that creatures are to be loved because what is truly lovable in them is an expression of the Creator's goodness.

9. This is a modern composition, for private or corporate use, based on several traditional morning prayers. Readers may like to use the blank pages at the end of the book for their own compositions.

10. *Altars*, p.42. The author imagines himself kneeling before the Cross, and hearing our Lord speaking these words to him.

11. From *Poems* 92 [iii. 24-7]. Almost every act through the day in Gaeldom was consciously offered, by many, to God. The habit of thinking of the Lord frequently throughout the day in connection with routine activities, helped to prevent that tragic division of the *wholeness* of life into so-called 'sacred' and 'secular'.

12. From *Poems II* [iii. 30-1].

13. From *Poems* 1 [i. 230-1]. The kindling of a smoored peat fire may seem to bear little resemblance to switching on an electric radiator: but its purpose — to diffuse warmth — is the same, and human beings still need to offer themselves and all their affairs consciously to God.

14. *Altars*, p. 146. This remark emerged, significantly, from a background of poverty.

15. From *Poems II* [iii. 316-17]. This grace again reveals that sense of the integration of body and soul as one unit which was characteristic of the Hebrews, and to which modern scientific thought is tending.

16. From *Poems* 71 [iii. 50-1]. Prayers were sung softly or said by men on their way to work, and this verse comes from one which was used by those who had much travelling to do — such as stewards, chiefs, and missionaries. Evidence for the fact that some people, even in the nineteenth century, were in the habit of using these poems or hymns throughout the day comes from various sources. In *The Catholic Highlands of Scotland* (Edinburgh and London 1909, p.75), for example, Dom Frederick Odo Blundell mentions Margaret M'Gregor, Glengairn, who 'composed and repeated constantly Gaelic prayers'. She was very much respected, and in the little hut which was her home she led a life of work, prayer, and great austerity, and often walked to a chapel nine miles away. And Dr Carmichael refers to a certain Somerled Maccalman who, in the oral tradition of the Gael, 'was always crooning these little hymns to himself' [note on iii. 54-5].

17. From *Poems* 443 [i. 332-5]. This is part of a litany used by a ship's crew before sailing. A form of this prayer was printed in Bishop Carswell's Gaelic Prayer Book of 1567.

18. *Altars*, p.60. A prayer of one who knows where his real value lies, that he was made in the image of God, and that Christ died for him.

19. From a leaflet about Mother Katharine produced by the Society of St Margaret of Scotland, Spital, Aberdeen. This Episcopalian Community was founded in the last century to work among the poorest, and Katharine Ogilvie spent her adult lifetime in Aberdeen's Gallowgate, then a notorious slum.

20. From *Poems* 38 [i. 318-21]. These lines were used by young fishermen who went out to make a catch for the widows, orphans and the poor at Christmas time. With their grasp of the wholeness of life, the users of these prayers accepted naturally the elementary fact that God is deeply concerned with our daily work.

21. From *Poems* 266 [iv. 62-7]. As all life is God's, the world cannot be regarded by a Christian as something for man's selfish exploitation. The reference to 'partnership' is significant.

22. From *Poems* 379 [i. 304-5]. The concept that Highland life of old, even after the rising of 1745, was simply a rural idyll, could hardly be further from the truth. The reference to 'busy-ness' should appeal to all who complain about modern life.

23. *Altars*, p.53. The tiller of the soil and the industrial worker — despite their obvious differences — have perhaps more in common than is often recognized. (This prayer is also suitable during Ascensiontide.)

24. The author, a native of Huntly, became a Congregationalist minister in England and later devoted his life to literary work.

25. *Altars*, p.47. This simple prayer shows how erroneous is the idea that religious consolation is reserved till after death. God offers joys as a foretaste of a fuller revelation of himself.

26. *Altars*, p.49. Uncomplicated simplicity. Cf. 'Truly, I say to you, unless you turn and become like children, you will never enter the kingdom of heaven' (Matt. 18.3, RSV).

27. From the *Lockhart Papers*, quoted in R. Chambers, *History of the Rebellion 1745-6* (London and Edinburgh 1869), pp.135-6. Men who could sweep almost any trained army off a battlefield in a matter of minutes also gave much evidence of honour towards enemies and gentleness. This is an eye-witness account of one such incident, reminiscent of the Good Samaritan.

28. *Poems* 87 [iii. 28-9]. This is in fact a rising prayer, but it is suitable — like many others — for use at almost all times. Intercession becomes so much simpler once it is realized that God 'knows our needs each one'.

29. From *Poems II* [i. 64-5].

30. *Altars*, p.99. Here is the only true security.

31. *Altars*, p.125. Joy is something much deeper than happiness. The pursuit of happiness and pleasure for oneself is not to be confused with that radiant joy which one often notices in Christians whose complete trust in God has apparently led to their ceasing to worry about themselves. God is the source of all true goodness; to acknowledge this is to step into a new and limitless experience of joy.

32. From *Poems* 326 [i. 38-41]. This poem was composed by a woman who suffered from leprosy, but was cured while she lived

alone by the shore on a diet of plants and shellfish. In Western Christendom a vivid appreciation of nature is frequently associated with St Francis of Assisi; but it was very marked indeed among the Celtic saints from at least the fifth century onwards.

33. *Hymnal for Scotland* (O.U.P. 1950), 758, and *The Church Hymnary* (O.U.P. rev. edn. 1927), 454, tr. Duncan Macgregor, 1854-1923. As in almost all primitive hymns there is a manliness here that is often lacking in later compositions. God is Almighty, therefore we can rejoice and set about positively grappling with life!

34. *Hymnal for Scotland* 756 and *The Church Hymnary* 53, tr. Lachlan MacBean, 1853-1931.

35. From [i. 4-5]. This is a short selection of Dr Carmichael's translations chosen by Adam Bittleston. Genuine attempts to spread the gospel are based on the fact that true joy only comes from God. The first three lines of the second verse sum up all our needs: an Almighty Father over the whole universe protecting us and therefore removing all fear; Jesus as our friend, companion and guide; and the Holy Spirit within us to strengthen — all One God.

36. From [ii. 158-9]. This type of prayer is very common, perhaps the best known version being the Irish hymn *St Patrick's Breastplate*. Our early missionaries seem to have spent little time in arguing with potential converts. Their approach seems to have been, 'You say you have power? Well, whatever you have got I bring a greater power — that of God, the Almighty Trinity'. (Cf. St Columba's visit to King Brude.)

37. From *Poems* 260 [iii. 86-7]. The more perfect the desire to fit in with God's will, the more is the heart open to the powerful influence of his Spirit.

38. *Poems* 48 [iii. 52-3]. An expression of an intense longing for one's life to be utterly given to God.

39. *Altars*, p.77. The reply of one famed for her gentleness.

40. From *Poems* 159 [i. 96-7]. A biblical religion is naturally full of scriptural words and phrases, such as 'Branch of Glory' for Jesus. In the severe poverty which was a major factor in Scottish life of bygone ages, the natural creative instinct and imagination of the Gael could find hardly any outlet except in an oral tradition of poetry and song. His highly developed sensitivity to nature finds expression in various ways, such as applying the term 'fragrant' to God.

41. *Altars*, p.101. A vivid plea to enter the great mystery which is at the very heart of the Christian faith, that 'God is love'.

42. An anecdote supplied by Sister Caroline, SSM.

43. From *Poems* 2 [iii. 40-7]. These verses come from a long prayer in which there may well be incorporated parts of a creed-hymn from the Celtic Church. This is surely the high water mark of devotion; and it has been said that no one can begin to understand the saints until he realizes that they are men and women in love with God.

44. From *Poems* 75 [iii. 176-7]. Those who try to face up honestly to their sinfulness find not a harsh God but a bracing gentleness and a hitherto unbelievable release through his forgiveness.

45. G.D. Henderson, *Mystics of the North-East* (Aberdeen 1934), p.116. Dr Keith was one of a number of Episcopalians who, in reaction against the church politics of the seventeenth century, placed a particular emphasis on personal discipleship in childlike (not childish) simplicity. They studied the spiritual classics, and this passage is taken from a letter to Lord Deskford.

46. *Altars*, p.129. Notice the word 'find' is not 'feel'.

47. *Altars*, pp. 95-6. No one can avoid the darkness of trouble. The serious follower of Christ is also likely to experience times of spiritual darkness when God does not allow him to be aware of the Lord's presence. Fortitude during these periods, expressed by faithfulness in prayer and sacraments and in trying to follow Christian moral precepts, enables a person to pass these tests of loyalty and to emerge strengthened.

48. This comment was made by one of radiant faith and courage. After at least a dozen major operations her condition was such that a further one, performed towards the end of her long life, though relatively minor, had to be carried out without anaesthetic.

49. *Mystics*, p. 74.

50. From *Poems* 101 [iii. 72-5]. God's presence must be taken for granted, whether or not we feel it. When it is not felt, God gives us the precious opportunity of making (often small) acts of trust.

51. *Altars*, p.81. If God permits the evil in the world to touch us, it will be in order to bring a greater good out of the situation. At times it will take very great faith to believe this. If we are growing in grace we are growing in faith, in our trust in God's goodness.

52. *Altars*, p.43. Its author writes: 'From a prayer — once her husband's — of a widowed woman who lived in the island of Mull.

This heart-cry broke from her almost every evening when she and her four children knelt together at the feet of God'. To call the Christian religion 'an opiate of the people' could not be further from the truth. The way of Christ is not some way of psychological escape, but the way of facing life and grappling with it.

53. From *Poems* 442 [i. 330-1]. Eastern Orthodox Christians are said usually to think of Christ as being surrounded by his apostles and 'the whole company of heaven'. As we meet him in the gospels he is most frequently in company, and many of these Gaelic prayers reflect this vividly, as the veil between the seen and the unseen world disappears.

54. *Poems II* [iii. 208-9]. This prayer can be adapted very easily for this age of road accidents.

55. *Poems* 317 [iii. 200-1]. For what purpose do we visit someone's house? To bring to them the peace and love of God?

56. *Poems II* [iii. 210-11]. Blessing — positive well-wishing — to- wards enemies as well as friends.

57. *Poems* 130 [iii. 206-7]. How often is it realized that 'goodbye' is a shortened form of 'God be with you'? And similarly with 'good morning' and 'good night'.

58. From *Poems* 405 [iii. 246-9]. This blessing, so rich in imagery, is of a kind that has been given by mothers who were to see their sons and daughters no more in this world. The remains of ruined crofts all over the Highlands and Islands bear silent witness to the thousands who have been forced to emigrate. Yet, in the Communion of Saints, for those who are 'in Christ', there is no real separation, either in this world or the next. For to be with Jesus is to be with all those who are with him, wherever they are. It has been said that, 'it is in this life that we make our friends, but it will be in the next one that we shall really enjoy them'.

59. *Altars*, p. 38. The essential time of stillness each day with Christ. Stillness of body; and at least attempted stillness of thought. The night is a natural time for this special daily trysting with Jesus, when the world is hushed — even to some extent in noisy cities. But some people prefer the early morning, or some other time. (It is surprising how ingenious people can be in order to make time for this, even in the busiest of days; it is a matter of priorities.)

60. This is a modern composition, making use of ideas and phrases from traditional Gaelic evening prayers.

61. From *Poems II* [iii. 256-9]. The whole prayer, from which these lines come, was used either individually or by the family together before going to confession. It is the Church's business to assure penitent people of God's forgiveness and to do this, where necessary, individually.

62. From *Poems* 3 [iii. 64-7]. This is a most valuable catalogue of sins for use in self-examination.

63. From *Poems* 167 [iii. 388-91]. True repentance — or being sorry because we have hurt God rather than being sorry for ourselves — always brings his forgiveness. To hurt a friend may cause a breach in our relationship, and we have to be reconciled. To sin is to damage our friendship with God; and to be reconciled with him necessitates first acknowledging our sin.

64. From *Poems* 158 [i. 96-7]. Daily thanksgiving for all these things is a necessary antidote to our taking them for granted — and finally forgetting God the giver. It is surprising, even on the darkest days, how much there is for which to be thankful. Things could be worse. To neglect gratitude is to avoid joy.

65. From *Poems* 165 [i. 90-1]. There is a story about someone who said, 'My religion is very simple: when things go well, I give thanks, and when things don't go well, I give thanks'. Gratitude helps to develop faith by drawing our attention to some of the many things that God is doing for us daily.

66. A tombstone inscription in Glenmuick kirkyard, by Ballater.
   Why does God give that natural love which is expressed in happy family life? Surely it is in order that love may spill over into the world around. There are many lonely people who would give anything for the smallest share in some family's life, some family's love.

67. From *Poems* 161 [i. 102-3]. God is almighty, so there need be no restriction in the scope of our intercession.

68. From *Poems* 170 [iii. 350-5]. The hearthstone 'was almost the altar-stone of the household', by which family prayers would be said. True love, being unselfish, does not include possessiveness.

69. From *Poems II* [iii. 356-7]. A very natural prayer at night when one's thoughts may well turn to absent friends and relations — and especially to those who are most loved or who are giving cause for anxiety.

70. Composed originally for the St Hilda's Church Guild of Prayer, Edinburgh. The word 'country' can be substituted for 'parish', when necessary.

71.　From *Poems*, p. 433. These verses are part of a long epilogue concerned with the life of Christ, and the Trinity.

The great Indian bishop, Azariah, once remarked that the question is not, 'Are you saved?' so much as 'Are you saving?' I am as much part of the Church as the clergy. My church will come alive just as much as I seek to pass on God's love. Every church is essentially a mission station. Is that true of mine? But no one can succeed in this except under the direction of the Holy Spirit and by his power.

72.　From the *Book of Deer*, tr. James Cooper in *Reliques of Ancient Scottish Devotion* (Davies 1934, p. 21). Deer was a Celtic monastery and later a medieval abbey in Buchan, Aberdeenshire.

To be increasingly on the side of goodness will result in an increasing awareness also of evil. The devil does not need to advertise his presence to those of Christ's soldiers who are not committed to battle.

73.　From the *Litany of Dunkeld* tr. *Reliques*, pp. 24-31. This litany was probably used and modified throughout several centuries by the Culdees.

In some ways life today has become easier than ever before. Perhaps it is therefore understandable that some people should expect the Christian life to become easier too. But in these days of 'instant coffee' there is no 'instant religion'. We may be able to control much of nature: to try to do the same with God is sheer impertinence. Modern education and life in general will be judged not least by their ability to produce men and women who have the stamina to persevere in Christian discipleship. Furthermore, this litany provides a reminder that divine charity and human compassion, though related, are not identical. The whole of this 'official' prayer of the Church breathes that spirit of triumph and joy which makes the primitive religion of these islands so attractive.

74.　From *Poems II* [iii. 264-5]. The Highland clans have been much maligned. A detailed examination reveals years of peaceful life; only an occasional atrocity, which was sung by the bards for generations owing to the horror it produced and which almost always was committed in hot blood rather than in cold; much chivalry, honour, and honesty; and the first Highland regiments winning admiration all over the world. These prayers emerged from such a background.

75.　This is the prayer used daily by those who support the work of the Sisters of St Margaret of Scotland in Aberdeen. Offering one's patient acceptance of pain or sickness or depression as a prayer for someone else, can convert a miserable situation into a mighty source of power for good; and we notice that Christ saved the world not so much by his preaching and healing, but by his 'converted' suffering.

76. From *Poems* 337 [iv. 274-5]. To pray for healing and to pray for God's will to be done, may appear at times to be incompatible, but God wishes the best for us. The best, for true well-being, may be physical health. Sometimes the best turns out to be the courage to face a sick condition. In the Church's ministry of healing either the one or the other gift is given; and sometimes the latter seems to be the greater miracle.

77. From *Poems* 338 [iv. 278-9]. Having prayed for others, we may then pray for ourselves — just the simple, natural requests of a child to its parent.

78. *Poems* 9 [i. 240-1]. In smooring, the embers were spread in a circle and divided by peats into three sections — one for each Person of the Trinity — and then covered with ash to preserve the fire overnight. Chores can be very monotonous. Jesus, as far as we know, spent thirty years living an apparently very ordinary working person's life. Mary was simply a housewife and mother, yet she is hailed as the greatest and most blessed woman in history.

79. *Altars*, p. 67. In this confused age we may well remind ourselves that it is the pure in heart who see God. Life's problems are then largely reduced to one major obstacle, our own sinfulness, which blinds us to the presence and clear guiding of God.

80. From *Poems* 105 [iii. 336-7]. This is part of a prayer for putting out the light. That all true prayer is inspired by God, and is indeed God praying in us, is a commonplace to Eastern Christians, but reference is rarely made to it in the West. Is it surprising, therefore, that many Western people reverse the biblical picture of the shepherd looking for his sheep, and imagine that they themselves — the sheep — are expected to search for Christ the shepherd? He is already in our midst, waiting to be accepted.

81. From *Poems* 515 [iii. 328-31].

82. From *Poems* 50 [i. 82-3]. The best comment on this type of prayer is in *Poems*, p. xxvii: 'This is the remarkable "lying down" theme, an extension of the Communion and Eucharist of the Last Supper to cover the hospitality afforded by God and Christ and the Holy Spirit to life's traveller or pilgrim: God is regarded both in himself and in his three Persons as a chief and

ard righ (high king), with personal ties to his people. It is after the manner of a chieftain ... and a more full version of the Communion or Agape of the Son of God. There is an immanence here; it is quite without parallel in English Christianity.'

83. From *Poems* 13 [i. 88-9].

84. From [i. 48-9]. This is from a prayer to the guardian angel, and the short compact verse can provide much fruitful thought for meditation.

85. From *Poems* 49 [iii. 312-3]. God's new covenant or 'new testament' — his promises in Christ — are the only true security.

86. From *Poems* 2. (see ref. 7 above).

87. From *Poems* 511 [i. 84-5]. When he goes to sleep, no one knows in which way he will wake up. This prayer is in marked contrast to that fear of even referring to death which the Orthodox Archbishop Anthony Bloom has noted, with much surprise, since his coming to Britain.

88. *Poems* 375 [i. 222-3]. Those who have experienced what became, in many parts of Scotland after the Reformation, a sabbath-black gloom on Sundays, will be agreeably surprised to discover from these traditional Gaelic prayers that 'the first day of the week' was regarded as a day of joy.

89. From his sermon when a new church was opened, quoted in J. Archibald, *History of the Episcopal Church at Keith* (Edinburgh 1890), pp. 82-4.
    Our need to arrive early for public worship and quietly focus our attention on God. A perfectly silent church before a service is a great blessing and, in eighteenth-century language, this prayer touches upon the kind of thoughts with which a wor-shipper might well fill his mind. Noticeably it emphasizes that we go to church to *give;* only then is the worshipper likely to *get* something of any real value at all.

90. From the leaflet *Holy Communion: suggestions for preparation and for use during the silences*, published by the Company of the Servants of God, and available at S.P.C.K. Bookshop, 7 Drumsheugh Place, Edinburgh EH3 7PT

91. From his *Life of God in the Soul of Man* (new edn., Aberdeen 1892), pp. 118-9. The Inter-Varsity Fellowship has recently republished this little classic by a young divinity professor which had a profound influence on John Wesley and others. The Christian life is essentially a corporate life, one of 'togetherness'.

The sacraments cannot be performed alone, and our Lord commands us to make use of them.

92.   From *Poems II*. How can people ever imagine that they are not in need of this?

93.   From the *Book of Deer* (see note 72). These sentences are taken from a thanksgiving which includes well-chosen verses from the Psalms.

94.   From *Poems* 190 [iii. 226-7]. A bridal song.
        When God is recognized as the source of all goodness, many other aspects of life fall naturally into their proper place, and with regard to sex, the tragic extremes of puritanism and permissiveness are both avoided.

95.   *Poems* 47 [iii. 200-1]. The translator comments: 'There can be few, if any, parallels to this baptismal sacramentaly of the Outer Hebrides.' At an infant baptism the baby would be passed round the whole congregation to emphasize everyone's responsibility in helping him to grow up as a Christian, fully integrated in God's family, the Church.

96.   *Altars*, p. 102. An old man watching children on their way home from school. The sense of the wholeness of life is vividly expressed here.

97.   *Altars*, p. 76. Do we pray for our children to be protected from life's troubles, or that they may be given strength to overcome?

98.   *Poems II*. [iii. 200-01]. A valuable little prayer for family use.

99.   From *Poems* 23 [i. 44-5].

100.   From *Poems* 28 [i. 132-3]. Note the whole of creation welcoming the Saviour.

101.   From *Poems* 80 [iv. 208-13]. These verses, so suitable for Palm Sunday and other occasions, come from a prayer for healing.

102.   From *Poems* 98 [i. 160-1]. A valuable weaving together of the themes of the Last Supper, the Agony in the Garden, and the Crucifixion.
        Those who lack familiarity with the Bible can have no idea of its inspiration and bracing effect. George Brown, a greatly respected Christian who died in a cottage near Crathie in 1828, was one of those who are really 'soaked in the Scriptures'; for 'with his Bible, both in English and Gaelic, he was so familiar that he could repeat large portions of it from memory, and rarely could a text be quoted that he could not instantly refer to its chapter and verse' (J.G. Michie *Deeside Tales*, Aberdeen 1908,

pp. 151, 160). One of the incidents which revealed his character occurred when his newly-wed daughter was drowned in the Dee, and someone inadvertently overheard his private praying by the river: 'She was my favourite bairn . . . but not my will, but Thine be done.' After this he took courage. For he knew that if God permits accidents, He also can over-rule them for good. And it is a Christian's business to convert evil into good, after the supreme example of Christ on the cross.

103. From *Poems* p. 189. 'In pasture isle or shieling far' can be replaced for urban use by 'in office block or factory floor'. Spiritual fellowship among Christians in industry can be very real, and of untold value in such matters as labour relations.

104. *Altars*, pp. 128-9.

105. From *Poems* 253 [iii. 88-91].

106. D.J. Mackey, *Bishop Forbes: a memoir* (London 1888), pp. 156-7. Alexander Forbes was a bishop of Brechin who did heroic work, originally single-handed, in the Dundee slums. His chronic ill-health resulted in his doctors ordering him abroad from time to time for recuperation.

107. This fuller version of a prayer which appears in the English Prayer Book of 1928, is thought by scholars to be the original form. I have not been able to trace its source, but those scholars who have been consulted believe it to be of Scottish origin. It is a favourite with many.

108. From *Poems* 531 [iii. 382-5]. These verses from a hymn of the professional mourning-women are not unlike the prayers which, in former ages, were quietly chanted by the person's soul-friend at his death-bed. The institution of the soul-friend was unique, akin both to a godparent, and also to the confessor of the Celtic Church from which it was derived. After the death, the soul-friend — though an outsider — would have a place in the deceased one's family. The office declined into that of the mourning-women, but the chants used seem to have remained much the same.

109. *Altars*, p. 92. Cf. a remark of the late Rev. Gilbert Shaw: 'At Communion God takes us in his arms and draws us to himself.'

110. *Altars*, p. 60.

111. *Poems II* [iii. 370-3]. In many churches — according to the custom of the apostles — the sick are anointed. So are the dying.

112. From [iv. 344-5]. The poem from which this verse comes is supposed to have been sung originally by a woman who had escaped the Massacre of Glencoe, but who assumed that in the snow she and her baby would die. Both however survived, after she had made this magnificent statement of faith.

113. *Poems* 449 [ii. 216-7]. Tides constantly go out and come in, but God is changeless. His immense love for each person, and his almighty power, are utterly reliable — as much in this present 'age of change' as in all other ages. In that central assumption of the Christian religion lies our security. Where there is real security there is no fear. When there is no fear people have a chance to live at peace with one another.

114. From [iii. 21].